Claude
MONET

Claude
MONET

by John Malam

Carolrhoda Books, Inc. / Minneapolis

Carolrhoda Books, Inc., c/o The Lerner Publishing Group
241 First Avenue North, Minneapolis, Minnesota 55401 U.S.A.
Website address: www.lernerbooks.com

Library of Congress Cataloging-in-Publication Data

Malam, John.
  Claude Monet / by John Malam.
    p.   cm. — (Tell me about)
  Includes index.
  Summary: A brief biography of one of the founders of the
Impressionist school of painting.
  ISBN 1–57505–250–4 (alk. paper)
  1. Monet, Claude, 1840–1926—Juvenile literature. 2. Painters—
France—Biography—Juvenile literature. [Monet, Claude, 1840–1926.
2. Painters.] I. Title. II. Series: Tell me about (Minneapolis, Minn.)
ND553.M7M286   1998
759.4—dc21   97–6618

Printed by Graficas Reunidas SA, Spain
Bound in the United States of America
1 2 3 4 5 6 – OS – 03 02 01 00 99 98

Claude Monet was an artist who painted in a new way. He didn't study a scene before painting it, but quickly painted what he saw. At first, people thought Monet's paintings were sloppy and unfinished. But slowly, they realized how talented he was. This is his story.

A picture of Claude Monet at thirty-five, painted by Auguste Renoir

Claude Monet was born in Paris on November 14, 1840. Paris is the capital of France.

When Claude was five years old, his family moved to Le Havre, a busy town on the northern coast of France. His uncle and aunt, Jacques and Marie, owned a grocery business in Le Havre. Claude's father went to work for the business.

Paris in Claude Monet's time

Claude went to school in Le Havre. He didn't like it. Years later he said, "School seemed like a prison and I could never bear to stay there, especially when the sunshine beckoned and the sea was smooth."

Modern
Le Havre

When Claude was a teenager, his teachers found that he had a special gift—he could draw. Claude liked to draw funny pictures of his teachers. He drew other people from Le Havre, too. An artist named Eugène Boudin saw Claude's drawings. Boudin thought the young man had talent. He began to teach Claude about painting. He often took Claude on trips to paint outside. By the time Claude was seventeen, he knew he wanted to be an artist.

One of Claude's drawings

Claude's father, Adolphe, didn't understand. He wanted his son to work in the family business. Claude's mother had died, so he asked his aunt Marie for help. She made Adolphe see what a good artist Claude was becoming. In the end, Adolphe decided that Claude could leave school and become an artist.

Claude painted this picture of his father and aunt at his aunt's summer house in Sainte-Adresse.

When he was eighteen, Claude went to live in Paris. He met many of the great artists of the time and learned about different ways of painting.

After only one year in Paris, Claude had to join the army. He was sent to Algeria, a country in northern Africa.

Claude in his soldier's uniform

Claude liked the bright, clear light of Algeria. The sun lit things in a way he had never seen before. He began to wonder if he could capture the look of sunlight in his paintings.

The next year, Claude became ill with typhoid fever and returned to France to recover. Claude's aunt helped him again. She paid a fee so he could leave the army. Then she persuaded Claude's father to let him return to Paris to paint.

Claude liked the bright light in the Algerian desert.

In Paris, Claude joined an artists' studio. The other artists could see that Claude's work was good. They liked him and he made many friends.

When Claude was twenty-four, he hurt his leg and had to stay in bed. One of his friends found a way to keep water dripping on his leg to stop the pain. Claude felt so much better that he was able to return to painting while still in bed.

When Claude hurt his leg, his friend Frédéric Bazille painted this picture of him in bed.

Claude's painting of the jetty at Le Havre

For a long time, Claude did not sell many
paintings. He was very poor and did not have
enough money to pay his rent.

Claude's family was worried about him. They
persuaded him to leave Paris. For a while, Claude
lived in his aunt's summer house by the sea and
painted some of the beautiful scenery around him.

In 1870, when he was thirty, Claude married Camille Doncieux. A short time later, the Franco-Prussian War began. Claude moved to London so he would not have to join the army again.

In London, Claude painted the River Thames. He liked the way it looked in foggy light.

Claude, Camille, and their son Jean returned to France the next year. At last, Claude began to sell his paintings.

Claude painted this picture of his wife Camille a year after they were married.

Claude called this picture of Le Havre *Impression, Sunrise*.

Claude and his friends held an exhibition in 1874. Claude exhibited his painting *Impression, Sunrise*. A writer who saw the show did not like the paintings. The pictures looked unfinished to him. He said they were only "impressions." The artists decided to call themselves "The Impressionists." Claude still didn't make much money from his work, but he kept painting.

Claude liked to paint the same view over and over again. He painted Rouen Cathedral more than twenty times. He wanted to show the building in different kinds of light.

Two of Claude's paintings of Rouen Cathedral. What differences can you see?

The Impressionist painters slowly began to earn respect for their work. More people began to buy the paintings.

In 1883, Claude moved to a big house in Giverny, a town near Paris. There he planted a beautiful garden. He said, "What I need most of all are flowers, always, always."

(Top and left) Claude's house and garden at Giverny

(Right) Claude painted many pictures of the bridge in his garden.

Claude Monet finally became famous, but there were many sad times in his life. His wife Camille died in 1879. His second wife, Alice, and his son Jean also died. When Claude was sixty-eight, he began to go blind. But this didn't stop his work. He continued to paint until he died in 1926.

People from all over the world go to art shows to see paintings by Claude Monet and other Impressionist painters.

Important Dates

1840 Claude Monet was born

1845 Moved to Le Havre

1857 Mother died

1859 Went to Paris to train as artist

1861 Joined army and went to Algeria

1862 Returned to Paris to study art

1867 First son, Jean, born

1870 Married Camille Doncieux

1871 Father died

1874 First Impressionist exhibition held

1878 Second son, Michel, born

1879 Wife Camille died

1892 Married Alice Hoschedé

1908 Eyesight started to fail

1911 Wife Alice died

1914 Son Jean died

1926 Claude Monet died

Claude in his studio

Key Words

art exhibition
a show where people can look at art on display

artist
a person who makes art, such as paintings or sculptures

Impressionism
a style of painting in which artists use dabs of color to show how a scene or object looks and how the light falls

studio
the place where an artist works

Index

Acknowledgments

The author and publisher gratefully acknowledge the following for permission to reproduce copyrighted material:
Cover Pushkin Museum, Moscow/Bridgeman Art Library, London
Title page Musée Marmottan, Paris
page 5 Musée d'Orsay, Paris/Bridgeman Art Library, London **page 6** Hulton Deusch **page 7** ZEFA **page 8** Musée Marmottan, Paris **page 9** Metropolitan Museum of Art, New York/Bridgeman Art Library, London **page 10** Musée Marmottan, Paris (*Monet in Algerian Uniform* by Charles Lhuiller) **page 11** Trip **page 12** Musée d'Orsay, Paris (*The Improvised Ambulance* by Frédéric Bazille) **page 13** Christies, London/Bridgeman Art Library, London **page 14** Musée d'Orsay, Paris/Bridgeman Art Library, London **page 15** Musée Marmottan, Paris/Bridgeman Art Library, London **page 16** Giraudon/Bridgeman Art Library, London **page 17** Bridgeman Art Library, London **page 18** (top) John Miller/Robert Harding Picture Library (bottom) K. Gillham/Robert Harding Picture Library **page 19** Pushkin Museum/Moscow/Bridgeman Art Library, London **page 20** Robert Harding Picture Library **page 21** Musée Marmottan, Paris

About the Author

John Malam has a degree in ancient history and archeology from the University of Birmingham in England. He is the author of many children's books on topics that include history, natural history, natural science, and biography. Before becoming a writer and editor, he directed archeological excavations. Malam lives in Manchester, England, with his wife, Hilary, and their children, Joseph and Eve.